The Elephant

Illustrations: Isabelle Raison
Text: Nadine Saunier

BARRON'S

New York . London . Toronto . Sydney

What is the largest animal that walks on earth?

The — a huge body

on four legs,
a very long nose that we call a trunk,
and two enormous ears
for fanning himself.

Some of the words in this book are replaced by pictures.
These pictures reappear and are identified at the end of the book.

The elephant has **4** large ivory teeth
and, on each side of his trunk, one
very long, very heavy, and very beautiful
tooth: the tusk.

The uses his tusks
to defend himself,
to lift up branches,
and to tear off tree bark,
which he then likes to chew very slowly.

Elephants

live in
When the males are ten or twelve years old,
they leave their families and
join the other young males within the herd.
Elephants are comical.
When they are on the move, the babies
hang on to their mothers' tails with their trunks.
While the babies play, the mothers watch over
them, because wild animals —
hyenas and

, are on the prowl,
waiting for a chance to eat the little ones.

The elephant is very strong.
He can uproot a tree.
He uses his trunk as
we use our hands.
This giant is so skillful
that he can take a bird's  from its nest
with his trunk.

The elephant bumps his forehead
against the trunks of trees.
The ripe fruit falls,
and the huge glutton feasts on it.

The  s, perched on branches,

are afraid of being shaken

off like s.

As soon as they see an elephant,
they run for safety.

The elephant disappears under water
just the way a does,

until only the end of his trunk is visible.
He spends hours showering
himself and walks miles for a

When he wants to frighten an enemy, the

flaps his ears,
lifts his trunk toward the sky,
and pretends that he's ready to attack.
When he really does attack,
he lowers his trunk between his legs,
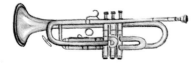 s, and charges....

It's very hot in the African jungle.
There are

many  .

To protect themselves from bites,
elephants use their trunks to splash mud
on their bodies. They

start out 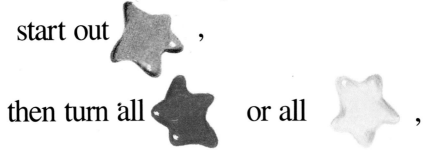 ,

then turn all   or all   ,

depending on the color of the earth.

A sick or

elephant is never abandoned.

Family members caress him with their trunks
and try to get him back on his feet.
Elephants live between sixty
and seventy years.
Man has long hunted elephants
for their tusks.
Today, hunting them is against the law.
They are our friends.